Monday

by Mary Lindeen • illustrated by Javier González

Content Consultant: Susan Kesselring, M.A., Literacy Educator and Preschool Director

magic wagon

Published by Magic Wagon, a division of the ABDO Publishing Group, 8000 West 78th Street, Edina, Minnesota, 55439. Copyright © 2008 by Abdo Consulting Group, Inc. International copyrights reserved in all countries. All rights reserved. No part of this book may be reproduced in any form without written permission from the publisher. Looking Glass Library™ is a trademark and logo of Magic Wagon.

Printed in the United States.

Text by Mary Lindeen
Illustrations by Javier González
Edited by Patricia Stockland
Interior layout and design by Becky Daum
Cover design by Becky Daum

Library of Congress Cataloging-in-Publication Data

Lindeen, Mary.

  Monday / Mary Lindeen ; illustrated by Javier A. González ; content consultant, Susan Kesselring.

     p. cm. —— (Days of the week)

  Includes bibliographical references.

  ISBN 978-1-60270-097-0

  I. Days——Juvenile literature. I. González, Javier A., 1974- II. Kesselring, Susan. III. Title.

  GR930.L563 2008

  529'.1——dc22

                    2007034063

4

Seven days in a week

are always the same.

The first day is Sunday.

What's the next one to name?

Which day of the week

is day number two?

It's Monday, of course.

Well done! Good for you!

Now, Sunday is the day
named after the sun.
Have you ever wondered
just what is a "Mon"?

It's not something tasty you eat with a spoon.

No, Monday is really named after the moon!

That's right! It was Moon's Day

in times long ago.

But then, we put it together

and stopped writing one *o*.

When Monday comes 'round

there's no time to sleep in.

The weekdays are here.

It's back to school once again!

14

Hello to the teacher.

Hello to your friend.

You have five days to learn
before the weekend.

On some special Mondays,

we stay home and play.

No work and no school,

it's a holiday!

Presidents' Day also comes

on a Monday.

We learn about George and Abe,

what a fun day!

What comes after Monday?

What day? Can you guess it?

Tomorrow is Tuesday.

You won't want to miss it!

The Days of the Week

1

Sunday

2

Monday

3

Tuesday

7

Saturday

5

Thursday

6

Friday

4

Wednesday

MAKE A MONDAY MUNCH

Have a special treat on "Moon Day" Monday. Have an adult help you spread soft cream cheese on a round cracker. Does that look like the moon? Take a bite. Yum!

MANY MONDAY MATCHES

Monday is the only day of the week that starts with the letter *M*. Think of other words that start with *M*. Play this game with a friend. Take turns saying *M* words.

WORDS TO KNOW

holiday: a special festival or celebration day, when people don't go to work or school as they usually would do.

tomorrow: the day after today.

weekday: any day of the week except Saturday or Sunday.

weekend: the days at the beginning and end of the week; Saturday and Sunday.